Kathryn Gahl writes about the unspeakable joy and pain of motherhood as she recounts a terrible loss, one that seems insurmountable. *The Yellow Toothbrush* is difficult to put down, the story so compelling that even after reading it, the narrative followed me for days. Read this book.

—Karla Huston, Wisconsin Poet Laureate 2017 – 2018

This miracle of a memoir takes its reader by the hand for a harrowing but heartfelt journey of redemption, mercy, regret, and love. *The Yellow Toothbrush* is a remarkable book that unflinchingly examines the challenges of motherhood, marriage, and family in ways I just haven't read before. A wonderful heartbreaker of a book.

—Nickolas Butler, author of *Shotgun Lovesongs* and *Godspeed*

Gahl's writing blends the natural world, the science of the brain, and the spiritual realms of loss. Her recollections of the cloistered universe of new parenting, the sexist gauntlet of high-pressure workplaces, the continual overleveraging of women to carry the lion's share of parenting and emotional burdens become bits of mosaic glass, sharp and bright. Here is a work of unsparing, visible truth.

—Katie Chicquette, poet and at-risk educator

Strong people tend to suffer in silence, but we all have breaking points. A tragic, honest, captivating, and essential read.

—Kate Porter, DO

With an artist's eye for the telling detail, a poet's gift for compressed expression, Gahl has created a work of transcendent beauty. We journey with her through a tragedy that has changed her family's lives forever, as she, her daughter, son, and other family struggle to make sense of what happened, to accept the crushing reality of their losses, to forgive, and finally to find glimmers of lightness and grace. This book is a triumph of human resilience and the power of Art to restore us to a deeper understanding of, and empathy for, all who carry a heavy burden of trauma through life.

—Georgia Ressmeyer, author of *Leading a Life*

I am forever changed by this story of love, grief, remorse, and perseverance. I couldn't put it down.

—Annette Langlois Grunseth, author of *Combat and Campus: Writing Through War*

Kathryn Gahl cannot change the past and all that has happened. The devastating loss. Subsequent losses. Generational losses. So she does what humans sometimes do when they come to the end of the rope. She lets go. In vulnerability she offers honest reality and promises for a just future.

—Kathryn Walczyk, Spiritual Companion

Kathryn Gahl's memoir reveals the deep reverberations of family trauma as she explores what happened when her own child committed an unimaginable act. Searing and soul-searching, it is an unforgettable meditation on love and loss.

—Theresa Kaminski, author of *Queen of the West: The Life and Times of Dale Evans*

Kathryn Gahl's elegiac memoir leads us as gracefully and assuredly as a dance partner into both shattering tragedy and the buoyant properties of love. Gahl examines the impact of an unjust system that funnels the mentally ill to prison, shedding light on the burdens borne by new mothers, and society's failed response to those in need of help. An elegant and graceful book, it does not shy away from pain or bitter truths, but rather, looks them straight in the eye.

—Nancy Dickeman, author of *Lantern*

Many of us will face unspeakable trauma in our lifetimes. How do we metabolize the pain and envision a life beyond despair? In this

memoir, Kathryn Gahl has given us a guidebook for the journey. With masterful skill, in language that is both sharp-edged and lyrical, the author bears witness to a devastating tragedy. Rendered through her cadenced voice as a storyteller, she presents an introspective view of a family *in extremis* as mother and daughter test the limits of love challenged by transgenerational trauma, abandonment, incarceration, and mental illness. Gahl's unflinching ability to stay with the darkest human feelings is a testament to an indomitable spirit and the impeccable fact of maternal love.
—Dale M. Kushner, author of *The Conditions of Love* and *M*.

The Yellow Toothbrush, inspired by family tragedy, may well be Kathryn Gahl's defining work. Through a mosaic of more than sixty interrelated poems, we travel on a painfilled journey of discovery, piecing together a narrative that will reveal that one life lost is never lost alone; the roots of suffering and remorse extend to all who loved them.   —Jeff Elzinga, author of *The Distance Between Stars*

This mesmerizing poetic memoir is a deceptively beautiful thing. The story will test your compassion and break your heart, but Gahl's writing, humanity, and capacity for forgiveness will lift you and heal you. Original and intense, this haunting narrative will stick with you long after the last page is read and the book is (reluctantly) closed.
—Patricia Ann McNair, author of *Responsible Adults*

Breathtaking in every sense of the word. A story of madness, of death, of prison, and of grief. But in Gahl's gifted hands, it also becomes a universal story of motherhood and of a love so powerful that it awakens each of us to the blessings of love and of luck in our own lives.   —Michelle Oberman, Professor of Law, Santa Clara University, and co-author of *Mothers Who Kill Their Children*

The severity of what happened—what is happening, to this woman, these women—corporealizes before our eyes. Yet we have no name for the genre here, nor should one call it hybrid, which would underscore the form of the work at the expense of its epic-like integrity. What I do know is this is an authentic masterpiece, matter and craft wrapped in a tight, symbiotic spiral, organic as a double helix.

—Karl Elder, author of *Alpha Images: Poems Selected and New*

In language both searing and plainspoken, Gahl illuminates the before and after, the shock and sorrow of a family tragedy. A clear-eyed, generous, and hopeful memoir, one that will remain with me for years to come.

—Sarah McCraw Crow, author of *The Wrong Kind of Woman*

Like the ancient epics, the images and rhythms of *The Yellow Toothbrush* take hold of the emotions like vise grips, making its insights into the human condition hauntingly unforgettable. Not reading for the faint of heart, this memoir takes a deep dive into psychic darkness, pathos, and tragedy but brings beauty and understanding out of brokenness and the incomprehensible.

—Kerry A. Trask, author of *Fire Within* and *Black Hawk: The Battle for the Heart of America*

In the work I do, I've known many traumatic stories like the one told in *The Yellow Toothbrush*, but the way Kathryn Gahl tells it invites a reader inside a harrowing experience while illuminating a great deal of love. Gahl takes particularly intense moments from her life, and tactfully wrestles them into art. This is Gahl's forte, the ancient art of healing through creativity.   —Brooke Laufer, PsyD

This masterful memoir tells a story that resonates with me as a mother who suffered postpartum depression and struggled with sky-high expectations coupled with limited support systems. The fragility of families and the enduring love between mother and daughter unfold with vivid detail. *The Yellow Toothbrush* is so deeply moving, so real, so powerful in its poetic language that it feels like the beginning of the way out of madness for all of us.

—Sylvia Cavanaugh, author of *Icarus: An Anthropology of Addiction*

The Yellow Toothbrush is difficult to read, yet hard to put down. Rife with sensory imagery, it relates a family's history, which culminates in tragedy, grief, anger, penitence, and finally reconciliation. Gahl's words are powerful, deeply felt, weighing the value of life possibilities and choices. —Marilyn Zelke Windau, author of *Adventures in Paradise* and *Momentary Ordinary*

Insights burn on the page in this eloquent exploration of a family's history and their many attempts to uncover where things may have gone wrong. Though lightened by humor and irony throughout, these are gutsy themes stared at unblinkingly. Yet one dances in the end. This is what emotional survival looks like.

—Vincent Eaton, author of *Intimate Dialogues*

Honest, heartbreaking, and visceral—yet written with an elegance, a poise that makes each complex iteration, each oscillation feel like a perfectly choreographed dance, *The Yellow Toothbrush* begins with a break (abrupt, shocking, painful) and continues to pull readers close in an irrefutable intimacy. Gahl refuses to let pain, fear, and shame define her story—or her daughter's—and she creates gardens with the brightness of bruises, earrings that shine with the ferocity of lightning, and a mother's love, bound yet never contained by prison bars.

—Emily Bowles, author of *The Satisfactory Nothing of Girls*

Once you start reading these short, evocative vignettes, you will not be able to put this book down. This memoir includes the tiniest of objects that make a life—the daughter's hoop earrings kept safely in the mother's drawer, the grandson's toothbrush still in its package, the weeds in the narrator's rain-soaked garden. Gahl's unforgettable memoir invites readers to deepen their compassion and "dance for everyone hurt, betrayed, or lost."

—Emilie Lindemann, author of *mother-mailbox*

Breathtaking, real, inspirational. In life, we plan, we prepare, we double-check our plans, and we imagine the possibilities. And then, sometimes, we find ourselves on a shanghaied journey—a journey we never imagined ourselves on. We don't know how we got there. We didn't buy a ticket. And we're unclear where the destination is. Follow Kathryn Gahl on her journey in *The Yellow Toothbrush* to find understanding, grace, empathy, and mercy.

—Dixie Zittlow, Senior Training Advisor for The Dibble Institute

The Yellow Toothbrush provides a rare glimpse into maternal filicide from the perspective of a mother and grandmother. She reflects on multiple losses: the loss of lived experiences with her grandson, the loss of her daughter, both physically and emotionally, and the loss of community support. Gahl also tries to make sense of how her daughter could have committed such an act by examining family patterns and the impact of a father's abandonment on a daughter. In the end, Gahl's resilience shines through, leaving readers clear that, however altered, her dance must go on.

—Cheryl L. Meyer, JD, PhD, author of *Explaining Suicide*

THE YELLOW TOOTHBRUSH

A MEMOIR OF TRAUMA AND MERCY

KATHRYN GAHL

Two Shrews Press

New York • Green Bay

Two Shrews, LLC
2550 Martha Avenue
Green Bay, WI 54301

First Two Shrews trade paperback edition 2022

Two Shrews and design are registered trademarks of Two
Shrews, LLC.

For information about special discounts for bulk purchases,
please contact Two Shrews Press at twoshrewspress.com.

Manufactured in the United States of America

9 8 7 6 5 4 3 2 1

First Edition

Library of Congress Control Number: 2022944402

ISBN 978-1-7338890-2-5

ISBN 978-1-7338890-3-2 (e-book)

Cover design by Kate Ogren and Laura Triechel
Book design by Kate Ogren

for Nora

There is always a wicked secret,
a private reason for this.

W.H. Auden
VII—from "Twelve Songs"

CONTENTS

PART ONE **BREAK**

PART TWO **MERCY**

PART THREE **MOTION**

PART ONE | BREAK

THE YELLOW TOOTHBRUSH

SUNRISE

The day after
I visit my thirty-six-year-old daughter

in prison
and see

> her auburn long hair severe in a bun
> > freckle-fair skin a ghoulish green
> > > big brown eyes pinched like a possum

I recoil

> and recall

that May sunrise
in 1977
when
hues of pink and purple
sparkled
on Lake Michigan
outside the window
of the room
where
a baby girl
whooshed from me

> a hush before the rush
> blood, sweat, and best-kept love

on a sun-blind morning
when the horizon line
moved

and I
became two

3

THE INSTITUTE

The day after
I visit my daughter in prison
I think about where she lives now, how I'll never see
her top bunk, a bony mattress missing her Dutch duvet at

Taycheedah Correctional Institute
ready at the edge of ridges and rocks

Taycheedah
from an Indian word that means camping place
a flat Wisconsin site chosen in 1921 for the
Wisconsin Home for Women—she had an eye for hanging paintings
in her condo, could do it without a measure or level—but here
the frame is the Niagara Escarpment
standing up
in relief
a prominent line of bluffs

with broken slabs
of limestone
toppled together
rimming the basin of a tropical sea awash there
400 million years ago.

How small I feel standing there.

Wind
skims the cliff, lofting, singing
with tribes on nearby Lake Winnebago long ago.

Walking toward the chain link fence
sounds rebound against walls in my heart:

Tell me, I ask, what is that curly barbed wire called?
Mom. Didn't you see *The Shawshank Redemption*?
No, maybe, I can't remember, I . . .
Razor wire. It's called razor wire! Anybody knows that.

Leaving, I approach the heavy metal gate, look toward the building
where I know a guard watches behind his shadowy reinforced
window.
    I wait.
Soon, a clanging bang opens the gate
    and I walk through, wondering

can she, can I
rise up, drum out the cynics, resist erosion,
gather chunks of loss
    like love notes I once put in her lunch box

find a place in the legend
of modern motherhood

    and let groundwater seep
through our stone faces
bring cooling relief
    beauty in
    brokenness, still
    life.

CLOUDY

The day after I visit my daughter in prison, temperatures top
out in the high fifties. Gray smears the sky. I dare to imagine the view
from her room. A window in the door
flickers fluorescent from spidery ceiling fixtures.

A small slit, five inches wide and fifty inches long,
gives a sliver of sun on a good day.
    She worked night shift for seven years, a tall and bright RN,
the one in the nursery who greeted every newborn with *Happy Birthday!*

    She may not see the landscaped moon for twenty-four years.

    By then, her night vision will cloud over with age.
    Mine will have joined the clouds.

SAY THE THING

There are days where
people who "know" look at me as if

perplexed   as if
I have one long nose hair
(though
not really—much worse)

shocked   as if
there's a nail in my forehead
(though
not really—much worse)

because when they hear of my daughter's
failed suicide.
They shudder, close down,
        cannot speak, vice-gripped between confusion and ignorance.

        Confusion means: I don't get this. I can't get this.
I do not want to get this. I won't get this.

        Ignorance means: why didn't she do this or do that
or this coulda been that—she coulda lifted her phone weighing
a thousand pounds and

6

called someone, anyone, and now, oh,   look   what's   she's   done!

Well, she's done   locked up
        and I'm left in a crater
                between confusion and ignorance.

                And it is called story.
                It shines by the light
                of my grandson, my sage.

He says, Spill, Oma.

He says gentle, fear, courage, guilt,
        help, believe.

He says
        Say the thing
        you cannot say

        to yourself.

THE STARS

The day after I visit my daughter in prison

I reel back
to a time of Lamaze all the rage

my perineum in purple power
as I push and push
feeling the pull, the draw, a vast favor
before
a resounding

IT'S A GIRL, head first

into the arms of her Papa
who wanted a girl
whose oil painting of a pensive redhead
done years before I met him
    resembled
    our daughter as an adult
    moody, brooding over this life
       what's the point

Six weeks passed
nursing my little redhead every three
    to four hours
the second-story bedroom our entire universe
her sausage-fat fingers gripping one of mine
    as I fed her the stars
      and myself too

And then, the opportunity
to go to the grocery store, alone,
bright light   the touch of melons
and tomatoes, people in colored clothing
whisking their carts, shouts down

an alley
of butchers   and floral stock
it was as good as going to Paris

BED

    The day after I visit my daughter in prison, I awaken
from deep sleep, eight hours of elusion. But I cannot get out of bed.

    I cannot remember what there is to get up for.

GARDEN

2

The day after I visit my daughter in prison,
my garden summons me beneath a sun hot and high
in September dry. It is Labor Day and I must labor.

I walk past a field of tall grass and purple loosestrife,
speculating how royal-colored elegance became so invasive,
impenetrable. Opening the garden gate,
I see busy weeds, the soil dark and wet
after last night's soaking rain.

I kneel,
begin the task of me versus quack grass.
My mound of pulled weeds grows.
Sounds of summer
linger: a coughing lawnmower, insect wings, whispers
of a far-off train, kids splish-splashing in a pool. Somewhere else,
a patio party spilling with beer and beef jerky.

Suddenly,
I miss all who have left such scenes—everybody
takes somebody with them—but I miss my grandson the most
his long curly eyelashes and jelly-belly laugh
suddenly no longer heard

after   something   inside   her   broke

while the cord connecting him with me tightens,
my toddler who would scurry to a crying child at daycare
and offer comfort, who ate slowly to savor each flavor,
including my Thanksgiving stuffing   and now his carbon elements
blow imaginary kisses, fill my earth-dirt hands, cushion my bony knees.

My spine curves and turns,
    each vertebra a celestial planet, unaware

how much longer it will spin. My spade glints in the sun
before it slides under the roots
and I tug, then yank—the release comes, the clump
of roots sticky with soil. I tap and whack them loose.
    I work past sundown, so late that I
look up to see a falling star, always a sign, right?

I've never been
    that good at sports
    but that star, I catch.   It is decidedly him.

HER YESTERDAY FACE

On this day after, I go it alone.   Avoid people.   Fear conversation.
Grow wary of meeting the horrified.
Other days, I might call my softhearted friends.

    This day, I embrace solitude.

And I think of inmates around us yesterday in the visiting room:
which one craves cocaine, who self-harms, will rethink drinking, who
can't read, who must parent from prison, who calls her a baby killer,
who eats entire bags of cookies and cheesy popcorn when canteen
arrives and then throws up, who murdered, craves a hug, cries every day,
is toothless, bribes another chick with butter pats, flushes the toilet
again and again in the middle of the night just to fuck with you, broke
down in Cage-Your-Rage class, or was caught loving another woman
and sent to THE HOLE.

    I think of my daughter fidgeting when the guard refused
to let her go to the bathroom—she, suddenly an animal
with one foot in a trap,
frantic for release like the fated night when neither outdated painkillers
nor a toaster in a bathtub
    electrified her wish
        to leave Earth.

And then I see her yesterday face once more, nervous and crumbling because one hour and fifty minutes are up and the ten-minute warning comes.

How I put on my coat and begin the carefully metered hug good-bye, our cheek-to-cheek kisses European style, her mouth caving, eyes flooding.

Don't do it, I say. Don't let them see you like that—you know what they'll do.

She stifles.

I go.

And today, all the tears she held in threaten me.

FOR WANT OF A RAINBOW

The day after I visit   my daughter   in prison,
the garden calls me again.
Like a slug, I go.

And no matter where I look
or what I do

I sense him as I turn the earth,
pull up roots of carrots and beans, once lush
        cucumber vines, shrunken and thin. And I

take them all—I who, too, have lost my roots—
        over the fence we go, tossed into fields wild
with memory of when I held him and he cooed,
infusing my flesh with rapture that knew no season,

that only knew a carriage for long walks,
longer naps, the baby yoga class
he and I went to, his breastfed fat cheeks flushing mine,
tummy time on a blanket on the grass
    and later, reading *Eyes & Nose, Fingers & Toes*
    how he pointed to each one

        and later

those same fingers held pieces of an organic carrot cake
she asked to bake
and I did   and he ate   with soothing yum-yum sounds
    at his first birthday

        and later

how I sang Kermit's *Rainbow Connection*
over and over for him
to calm fussiness

        And

            and

                and

those swims next summer where we hoped
    to float, pay no heed to gravity,
    the tug of each day's passing.

GROWING ODDS

There came a day
I assume I took a pill
except I don't take pills
    though it
    looked like a pill
    round, no not exactly, more
    elliptical and crimson
    like a tipsy sun after
    a beer-lit late evening
and yet I knew it wasn't a pill
for I don't take pills
(it bears repeating) though I
take vitamins—she did, too: fenugreek seed and fennel
    to keep up her milk supply because she lacked sleep
        and
    colleagues chided her about pumping and
    the fiancé said he wanted his son off the tit
while she flowed and pumped against growing odds.

The vitamin I took on the other hand
addressed the degeneration of eyesight
and I was degenerating, I was sure.
My hope, my need to regenerate
loomed large and in no time, I felt like I had grown
two heads.

That felt good. It brought perspective.
I needed perspective: a new angle, the lens
    of an all-knowing narrator
    who would build a story with an ending
I could live with.

And so I hoped to grow another head.
That way, I would see in 3-D.

LIST

The day after I visit my daughter in prison, I make a to-do list,
mostly for something to do.

If she made a list, it would not list things to do.
It would be called All Things Lost.

No paper stretches far enough
for such a list in the teeny tiny cage she shares.

So I stretch for her, naming
fireflies and firecrackers
bicycle rides and Riesling
slip-and-slide and summer peaches
porch swings and a lover's kiss
The Best Chicken Piccata In Little Italy
lifeguarding and all things purple
the High Line
tennis and foot massages
service work in Jamaica
eating pannekoeken in Amsterdam
cruising Amtrak in the Rockies
Victoria's Secret
buzzy, spy-themed birthdays in a Milwaukee tavern
horseback riding and homemade bread
bear hugs, treasure hunts, Whole Foods

and footnotes

for speeding tickets
and hangovers
the stuff of fine story

Perhaps she would add
a lucent yellow toothbrush

she bought for her son, anticipating
how in a few months she would teach him
    to brush his own teeth.
        On the handle it has soccer balls
        in colors of blue, red, and orange. Happy colors.

I have that toothbrush, unopened. Therefore,
        it does not
        make the list
        of All Things Lost

REJECTION

3

The day after
I visit
my daughter   in prison

I try to reach out, yet how do I chronicle
what I cannot see
when strangeness lines my lexicon

The prism of pain is what makes a prison,
not the penitents, punishment,
but a future devoid
of hugs and touch, how one cellmate rips off another's sugar,
a claim my daughter stole the scent out of the hair gel, mayhem
when one punches another, forbidden caresses in the shower nonetheless

    all of it

    stranger than a stranger in a strange land
    stranger-anxiety
    stranger than fiction

I use the word strange a thousand times
    forward
    backward
    tossed
in a circle
in a thousand sentences
as if practice makes poetry
as if cures will emerge from upgraded labels
like Perinatal Mood Disorder, shards of it
scattering like white light in a prism
    The Worry
    The Dread
    The Panic

factors of modern motherhood blending with
anxiety, depression, sleep-hunger, and perfectionism
how this can start during pregnancy and implode after giving birth:

the puzzle put together by Phillip Resnick, MD,
    a forensic psychiatrist who interviewed her for
    six hours
        while she was handcuffed, ankles shackled
            to a chair in the Milwaukee County Jail,
                a Velcroed suicide suit
                  her only jail garment, stiff and cold,

to keep her from danger, from damage already done:
    intolerable misery that
immobilized her, froze her when the fiancé's leaving
    stirred up memory in her muscles and
    her tongue—how even as a child
she could not find her feelings,

could barely speak

    after her Papa ran out, literally disappeared
when her brother was nine
and she was twelve, entering the minefield of seventh grade.

Her brother required crutches,
conversion syndrome it's called, a return
    to toddlerhood
        where   he
            needed help
                to balance
                    to put
                one foot
                    in front of the other
And she clamped down, eyes darker than a wishing well. She did
    everything not to break

into tears, thinking Papa left because she was 'difficult.' I hugged her.
Her arms hung limp, worn-out rubber bands.
The bones in the back of my neck tightened.

I could not face fate and she could only stare at television as though
it were a genie, releasing magic mixtures of hope.
    That first Christmas, she
    decorated our home

when I could not,
when she surely felt the weight of the household descend on her,
when she surely spun my sense of abandonment into her own

after her Papa's hot-headed split led her to believe
    she was
    "globally unlovable"

    is what Dr. Resnick wrote in his forensic report.

    It sounds crazy, childhood traumas, rolling tornadoes and hailstorms
from Papa's moods, memories of his outbursts stored away
safe as cement in the Georgian brick house where Mama rebuilt a home
until circumstances bust open
    her subconscious neurology and
        blast a cannon of panic,
decades-old rejection stored in the hippocampus,
    deep-rooted, wary on a subliminal level of desertion
    that would mimic her father's flaming, crazymaking exit

I-don't-know, I-don't-know, became her refrain
way back then . . . the shame of a misfit . . .
a preteen with a father

who went so far afield, he landed in another country

while a murky undertow

snagged her. My son. And me
as I held on to my nurse-manager job,
our home, home-cooked meals every evening, crying for public decency,
my dream of becoming a writer derailed

while a lyric stuck in her head for decades,
something I realized when the public defender asked her
to make a statement at her sentencing, and
all she could say was

I don't know how this happened.
I don't know.
I don't know.

STAYING POWER

For days after I visit my daughter in prison
I am under a veil
of thick dim sky.

I am pale with thunder.
I am electrified with lightning.
I am white with rage.

Still, I can neither drown betrayal
nor make a snow monster
out of crystal white
glittery nothingness
so needed
this warm December
to block the roads
close the stores
huddle us
around the Jotul stove
      like in the early years

when we lived on five acres in Wisconsin's rolling hills
in a century-old farmhouse we renovated, grasscloth wallpaper
in the living room, a staircase her Papa opened from a narrow rise,
red ceramic tile in the kitchen.

Outside, a brick walk he artfully laid, and
a garden he crafted, 40 x 60, enough food to feed
an entire threshing crew,
an old tiller he wrestled before he dropped on his knees with bean seeds
and hollyhock seeds, a sunny disposition
each time he went to the garden to tend it, speaking to my bulging belly,
    The child in there is driving me, he beamed
and later, birch trees planted for that child and the second one too,
a rope swing on the oak tree and
a curly black sheep
named Lamb Chop

    Mama Bear, Papa Bear,
        and two little bears, red-cheeked from sledding
        kneading whole wheat dough, playing with puppets
        and Play-Doh
    Papa's carved chess set ready for when they were older, he said,
        but for now, finger painting, Discovery Toys, and
oodles of library books, including

        Good Night Moon read
        under a six-foot square skylight
        ample with moonlight

any glow would help
for he had a darkness about him
different from other dads
fastidious about his clothes, did not like to socialize
yet when he did, could be charming and funny
And all of it crafted into a Christmas card
        a family together
        in a picture-perfect moment

holding a song book and belting out tunes
    looking good
    no hint of Papa's
        restless impulsive self

    nor of Mama's staying power
    to a fault

EARRINGS

The day after I visit my daughter in prison
I think
of her pierced ears

that photo on the balcony
in sunset when
her long hair

fell in twentysomething waves from
the jaunty black bowler hat
she wore, silver hoop earrings

in the pierced holes
of her lobes
how in a few years

she added a hole
in her nose, the sparkly
diamond stud that made her

brother laugh when he saw
it, *makes your nose look bigger,*
he said, and so in time

the nose hole grew back and
now when I visit her

I imagine earrings dangling
rings on her fingers
and toes, the belly button
stud dazzling in summer heat

but all the holes
have grown back
and her sexy hoops
and little pearls and
diamond ring are here
with me in a drawer

in the hole in my heart.

IN HER BRAIN

The day after I visit

> my daughter
> my DAUGHTER
> MY daughter

> in prison

her words at my skull, how she told me
she was in the Milwaukee County jail
for a week

> before

she realized her son was dead:
I knew he was gone somewhere
but I figured he'd come back.

> my daughter
> my DAUGHTER

    MY daughter
her brain changed, a mishmash of cognition and memory rearranged,
edge-walking through neurobiology as
billions of neurons interlace anxiety
and hypervigilance, gobble up sleep. Twenty percent of women
experience this stark alteration; brain-imaging tools
can measure new motherhood's gray matter, her confusions and dismay
when connections clog, synapses snap.
On this day, I am not a new mother nor am I sleep-deprived
Yet I too
figure he will come back.

O Goddess of Sky and Sea
deliver him to me.
And I will hold him safely.

4 STUFF LIKE THAT

The day after I visit my daughter in prison

an email pounds the air like
    a cave man
    come for a clubbing:

> I am afraid to ask this but will go ahead:
> have you ever felt angry with your daughter?
> To be honest, I have.

I read the email.   I print it.   I post it on my wall.

The writer, five states away, feels anger toward someone she never met.
Ok. Sure.
Her question addles me.

Anger. Hmm. I should find some, should I not.
See red. Twirl purple. Turn green at the sight of friends' grandbabies.
Drink till I dehydrate. Vomit.
Or, try a timeworn form of anger—hurt someone.
    Those who hurt, hurt, it is said.

    My anger simmers. Anger is a secondary emotion, easier to reside
in than the primary surge of grief and fear—I learn stuff like that now.
And so, my anger cooks, bubbles, and boils.
It looms like the apocalypse.

It seeks to cleanse and uncover

    the mother who blacklisted her for a third-grade party
    the junior high harasser who crimped her finger in the locker
    the Papa who left
    the family who
    the family who
    the family who
    the Papa who didn't pay child support

her bad boyfriend who burned my clutch
her next sweet talker in jail

her friends who
her friends who
her friends who

the I-love-you but I-gotta-go Papa
her kisser whose teeth fell out from lack of brushing
her therapist who said she's smart, she'll figure it out
the I'm-so-BUSY who
the I'm-SO-busy who
the I'M-TOO-BUSY-TO-CALL-YOU who
the home inspector who masked the bathroom mold in his report
the contractor who screwed up the bathtub fix
the day care she reported when her son went missing for five hours

the colleagues who
the colleagues who
the colleagues who

the Peaceful Parenting Blog she read and he wouldn't
the lactose-free milk he balked about buying when she weaned
the arguments over cry-it-out or hold-out-all-night
the doctor who said
the doctor who said
the doctor who said
the Copper River salmon versus Tombstone frozen pizza
the stroller and Pack 'n Play she put together, alone
the TV screen serving up dinner

and her boss, a surgeon with a stony mask
his supporting role in this story

TOUCH OF GENIUS

Consider the keystone of all this. Her Papa:
locked away
in the mind of his eye
looking to escape from
his daughter, son, and me

lured by social benefits in his native Netherlands
and convinced he did not have long to live,
he worked like a dervish conjuring up
watercolors, refined and nearly angelic
     painting
without worry over car payments or rent or bread

a touch of genius, wrote one reviewer, one can see it with the freedom of
the line, with his use of the brush, and of course with the colors.

His Aunt was surprised he once held a job or two. He's not meant to work,
she said with conviction, an artist willing to go without friendship and love,
emotional pain his constant companion

     a man blinded by his own light, by
a sensual state of DNA
left in the hollow of our children's marrow
when shadows of painting and parenting
     advanced and receded
     he tried and quit,
     tried again,
     unsteady with hues, whether red or purple with tints of black and
blue mad desires of his melancholy
     and then—
     fate whacked free will one day

during a family vacation when he tossed me the car keys and sauntered
across a bridge in the Wisconsin Dells, stealing away to a fuzzy future.

I threaded my fingers into my daughter's hand on one side, my
son's on the other, and we saw him fade into a speck.

In time, cards and letters
played like a broken-record

    I miss you

             I miss you

                    I miss you

    I miss you

                     I missssss

UNDERWATER

Decades before I will call my daughter prisoner

her father and I lay on a Workbench bed,
big as a boat, floating from first touch
to sometime past noon in Greenwich Village
breezes. A skyscrapered sun splashed our deck.
Vivaldi drowned out the West Side Highway.

It was a cove called hope the Dutchman and I
climbed from. He was 32 and I was 25, roaming
fruit stands and wine stores, tacking between drivers and loads,
waving at Johnny and his faux auto repair
fronting the numbers.

We plied past
galleries that did not sell his watercolors

and made it to the bread store where the day half-done
smelled like home. Brioche and croissant went into one bag,
peaches and raspberries another. We bought cognac
on credit

and lollygagged back for hips and handplay
and, afterward, peches melba.

We played that scene and it played us
with half-mast fantasies of Grand Marnier,
linen shirts, soft leather
shoes, boeuf bourguignon, past balances due.

Four years later, we made one baby, then another. And soon

he traded his brushes for a deck of business cards,
new titles every couple of months, always a reason
to quit, commit the boss.   I scavenged for self-help
books, prayed for better weather,

and deluded myself
until that summer vacation when
he ran aground, sleepless and manic. And disappeared.
The cops in the Dells couldn't find him. The one cop in our village
couldn't either, couldn't know he had hitchhiked home, taken our
other car, a Peugot,
drove an hour south, and rented a room in a widow's house.
From there, he called, asked us to bring him some items.

We went,
my son clinging to me,
my daughter refusing my hand
walking like a stick figure.

Several weeks later, he disappeared again, the Peugot found
at the Milwaukee airport.
At first, he mailed postcards from Florida:
I love you. I miss you. I'm trying to figure it out.

Come home, the children said, and he did—for a week—then
disappeared again, longer, weeks of forever with book bills due

and a rummage sale to buy school clothes while the baffled village cop
scratched his head and kept asking if I was safe.

I was.
The danger was not inside me.

Then, he mailed an 8 x 10 of himself sunning on Canary Island,
birds of every color on his head and arms, and the kids and I
wondered who took the photo,
did she know we were strapped for school clothes and milk, did she know
he desired a patron, a Renaissance supporter of the artist.

Months trawled along and became years, my nights too long
after our daughter's first date, first unease, our son
begging for soccer cleats.

After a decade with him in his Holland, me in America,
he phoned from the end of earth, cancer.
The pounding sea parted, he waved
brilliantly, madly,
and cried through fiber optics on the ocean floor—

Please come. Please.

And then dial tone, a shell at my ear, an echo of our beginnings,
the early chaos we loved to hear.

Our daughter and son, by then young adults, flew across
the Atlantic to say good-bye to what
was left of him, cancer chewing his brain.

They returned home and several weeks later, he sent me an invitation:

Ik wil je graag uitnodigen voor een
afscheidsbuffet op zaterdag 13 mei 2000,
op 'Het Oude Slot' te Heemstede om
17.00 uur tot ca. 20.30 uur.

In English, he had written:

I would like to invite you to a farewell dinner
on Saturday May 13th at the Old Castle
from 1700 – ca. 2030.
My meaning is to hug each other to share the friendship and intimacy.
Feel free to give a speech or read a poem and if you play an
instrument
I would appreciate it all.

The last entry on the invitation
Laten we vrolijk zijn en nog van elkaar genieten
means this:
Let us be happy and
enjoy each other company
in this little time.

My turn to fly. I pushed his wheelchair to his
living funeral with Dover sole, white asparagus,
andijviestamppot of Dutch endive and potato salad, and
juicy fat strawberries—none of which he could eat as
people bid him farewell with piano solos, guitar, poetry,
his hot-blooded watercolors on display and
so many pretty women
in warm wet tears.

I told him good-bye, arranged for his ashes to be near us.

On a bright sunny day,
our son lowered the urn into Kohler soil,
our daughter tucked her sealed
letter beside it. And then a rose,
from each alone, atop
the dirt while Pachelbel played tranquil, white tones.

Some days I smell his cooking.
Some days my two adults crave more memory.
I know now how buoyant we become
when found, how to breathe underwater,
how not to drown.

5 SHARP TURNS

The day after I visit my daughter in prison
I hug her brother

squeezing what feel like total-body blisters
wanting to kiss bruises and dab baggy damp eyes
help helpless hopeless historical wounds

but it is a seething scene
for us—the agony, stabbing
    —we are numb
    —dazed by disbelief

We hug some more
who starts it and who ends it,
that's a fair question
    and we don't need an answer, we have lived so many
questions and taken, as he says, so many sharp turns and This One

body-slams me back to where
    over two decades ago
we three fell together like a tripod, bracing,
while I raised them alone after their Papa disappeared.

Back then, I did what I knew
    and what I didn't
    know I did anyway
    moving from fear
    of loving them too little
    to soccer balls, tennis rackets,
    and shoes that made me
    jump higher on the fifty-hour career ladder
    when all I wanted to do
    was sit in the sandbox
    and build castles

because I wanted to believe
I was the architect
of color and design, architectural line
I wanted to believe I could
reshape them and
make something of myself.

NIGHT NURSE

She was a night nurse.

And mindful
of blurry biorhythms,
she packed snacks, marking
what time each item would
stave off sleep. Then, she
double-locked her door,
scraped newfallen snow
from the windshield, and
counted stars on the drive
to work. It was time to turn off
the ignition but she sat there,
listening to rap music.
Within the throbbing, she heard
the lub-dub of her heart. She
was single, thirtysomething,
anxious to love and be loved.
Notes bolted from her chest and
drummed in her ears, blood rushing
in tribal rhythms, women
bursting to birth, mothers too
tired to breastfeed. She kept
going into night after night
kind and confident
recording newborn names
Hudson, Emma, Leni,
cradling babies in the nursery
exuberant, a calling—
what would she name hers
some day but until then
each amazed baby face
would hear her
whisper

Happy *Birth* Day!

SERENITY

Night slid in slowly
that Sunday in March

winds dying down on her
driveway frozen in ice

that would melt tomorrow
the blizzard grip giving in

after the fiancé's abandonment
and me as morale booster

showed up for listening
laundry, lunches, vacuuming

and then kiss-kissed her goodbye
hair strewn around her drowsy face

kiss-kissed him goodbye
under a halo of light from the lamp

before he returned to the breast
nourishment private and tender

the two tangled in need
and joy as I closed the door.

It would be the last time
I saw them together

snuggled on the sofa
Madonna and Child

in soft serenity.

6 BREAK

The day I visit
my daughter   in prison

I don't think about the scanner

> or the command to turn my pockets inside out
> prove I am not wearing a watch
> or an underwire. I do not even think
> about four heavy metal doors
> locking hundreds of women
> in the purgatory of punishment

as I walk closer to hugging her in that penal colony.

I think of the word *break*.

She once broke out with acne.
She never broke a bone.
When her car broke—blew a head gasket—well, so did she.

Still, she refused to break at her Papa's funeral
    years after I found him in the Netherlands
    with a transatlantic phone call

> *What* were you thinking?
> I'm a lousy father. Best if I just disappear.
> Not. Not best at all. The worst. The worst!

I handed the phone to my then nine-year-old son. The air felt heavy
and tight and I worried this prickly phone call would sweep his asthma.
    Papa, where are you?
I didn't hear the reply but I knew Papa, birthed in wartime
and hard-wired to be scared, didn't know where he was, either.

36

It would take time for him to find himself and in due time, she,
indignant and anxious, hoping to find herself, went to live with him
for a semester, studying at the International School of the Hague.
Then, strained summers for her and her brother under Dutch skies
before their Papa came home to America in an urn,
his fourth and final disappearance.

And when, on the dark side of midnight, her fiancé
stormed out, what went before
went ahead, knotting her plea . . .
Please, Please. Don't leave me.

But he did, leaving the Valentine's card where he wrote
The Only Thing I Hate Is How Much I Love You

And when he left, he left
toothpaste he had smeared on the mirror
kitchen garbage cans he turned backwards, making the
foot-pedal inaccessible as she held the baby

super-scrubbed floors
organic baby shampoo
bags of frozen breastmilk

day care, night care
the mortgage, rusty lead pipes
promises to fix a deck, leaky water heater, congested
faucet, loose storm door, a lot to learn within walls of mold
in a house with
windows and doors
from mid-century
crazed by blizzard cold and winter bluster.

And when the frosty side door banged
the last time, she called, breathless and vexed,
and I calmed her, this, our time-worn pattern.

Only this time, I failed her—failed to parse jagged parts, to
sense the fire, flint, call it what you will—a wildfire in her that would
burn both past and future,
leave a mound of ashes after sacking her dreams, yet igniting the
search engine on her iPhone which later would reveal
                                        to detectives
                    the *exact* minute she Googled

                    WAYS TO DIE

                    signals that would be read
            by a forensic psychiatrist from Case Western
                    who for thirty years studied
            causal relationships in something called
                            filicide
                    a word punched in my face

                            after

            the whirring chaotic clatter of the night
                        she fell

and

                kept
                    falling
                            and
                                falling
                                        and

the next day
got up
took her son to daycare

drove to work
and
put on a white lab coat embroidered with her name, BSN, RN

smiling
at patients and staff
similar to what I had done
years ago

terrified
of what might come next

though I was
neither drained by breastfeeding
nor battling custody

And as she said, later much later,
I couldn't do what you did, Mom

WORD SOUP

I ate alphabet soup as a child and raced ahead in the second-grade spelling workbook, consuming one new word after another.

Years later, I sampled a word a day to expand my language, reading "30 Days to a More Powerful Vocabulary" during lonely nights in Boston.

But in all my decades of word learning, I never knew the word filicide. Now, I do.

BEARING WITNESS

Cheryl Meyer, Wright State researcher, finds
maternal filicide
comes from a complicated life
wrought with pain and rejection by men

a real or believed lack of social support
plus a struggle
with one's own demons.

Sir Francis Bacon believed
knowledge is power.

I believe both Meyer and Bacon.

And
I believe
in bearing witness

to tell this story
or the crush of expectation
will happen elsewhere
differently
but the same.

I have witnessed its bricks, how it is built.
Dreams.
Devotion.

And then fights
collapse into ferocious commotion
until
tomorrow is frozen.

WITH OTHER MOTHERS

The day after
I see all the daughters
in prison

I pray for
every mother
with a daughter in prison

for every grandmother and great
grandmother whose arms cradle a ghost

Where are these women
made of umbilical cords
woven with courage and resolve

who gave birth without anesthesia
who made costumes and knot rolls
whose bread rose like a lyric

the brave new makers of meaning
who braided hours of despair
terrified by the dark as they twisted toward dawn

Some went mad
        insults, expletives, vitriol
some lost touch
        bitten nails, broken hips, heartsick

And still others stay present with me
like at swimming lessons, attentive
determined to not miss a thing
and nonetheless forced to imagine

a hive abuzz, straw eyes, sand mattress, nonstop constant count
lockdowns and pepper spray, med-pass in gray light
tornado drills (put your mattress over your head)
crud in the drain, ant infestations, toilet paper rationings (use a sock)
stingy heat in winter cells, no AC in summer steam

And so, stand tall, I say, to every mother in ricochet.
Put on your armor. Steady your gaze. Seize your mouth harp
and make it yowl, piercing the drums
    of powers that be
until they exercise the greatest power—mercy.

PART ONE | BREAK

THE YELLOW TOOTHBRUSH

PART TWO | MERCY

THE YELLOW TOOTHBRUSH

7 WITHIN AND WITHOUT

I worry.

Because yesterday, half an hour into my visit,
my daughter asked to go to the bathroom
> and
> was
> denied
> access.

The visit just began, said
the C.O. with bottle-blonde hair
piled atop her head. Positioned
at an elevated desk,
she declared my daughter
> could pee
> one hour
> into the
> visit,
> not one-half hour
> and if
> she wanted
> to pee at the half-hour
> mark
> > the visit would end.

I asked my daughter, Why?
She shrugged, lowered her eyes
like a scared dog.

I cannot erase the image of my daughter
wiggling and fidgeting,
a five-year-old trying to hold it,
hold it
> crossing and uncrossing
> her legs

47

twisting from side to side
   squirming

Oh God
I am going to wet myself
she sighs
she sulks
I can't concentrate on what you're saying
I have to go so bad

And whether she dribbles, I don't know.
There is much I don't know.

Ceiling fans slap the air.
Vending machines purr.
In her state greens, she is a pallid lichen.

As for me, I must not worry
   this day after

I must conjure up
   a shape-shifting water spirit
   to wash over her

radical drops of radiance
painting her cheeks

   her lips dammed-up
a turbulent river taking over
her lanky, long spine

lifting her

      a million tons of wind and rain
      at her back

      a change of direction
      within and without

THE NEVER-ENDING EXPLANATION

The day after I visit
my daughter   in prison
there is a thief at my door.
    Grief.

It is a slow note.
It is a sponge twisted until the water runs out
    the chip on my shoulder
    the can I kick.

All day long mournful sounds
    why didn't I know?
    what could I have done?
    what should I have not done?
    how come no one knows
        when danger is planted,
        what makes it sprout?

I scour the history for signs, states of mind.
I watch their story
    and it watches me
blistering and off-key
she as mother and he as father in thoroughly modern America
    sinking, she scrubbing floors at midnight, he asleep
at his homework computer, the baby's ear infection brewing,
Daddy's exams due, snow swallowing the house, laundry to shovel too,
Marlboro Reds on the stoop, a Daddy door slam after every smoke.

    I am going to lose my mind, a text found
    in the aftermath with her friend texting back
    Wow! You have a lot on your plate.
    Let me know
    if you need anything.

Anything. What did Anything look like? Get up? Get at 'em? Just Do
It? One more text message? What did Any Thing want?

One thing.
Let Mommy sleep!

I shrivel and
shrink the way dreams shrink
upon awakening . . .   to the realization

life will never be
as it was
life will be as it is
as feelings become facts

as I find my way
through rock-strewn times

after she smothered her beloved baby boy
"an act of altruism"
the forensic psychiatrist wrote
explaining like Medea what cannot be explained, really

she herself believing:
I did the right thing
because
now no one can hurt or disappoint him

her childhood scars twisted tight
bolts
of voltage zapping her brain
when she reasoned
she could
break the cycle of broken

"Please don't go, I'll eat you up, I love you so"
wrote Maurice Sendak

she could not find such truth
nor a way to express shame and silence

nights all alone
whether alone with someone else or
alone-alone
both a state
of sleepless disconnect
mother-love falling off the edge of dawn

and grief
rising
to the profound
deep

ENTERED

Months into the investigation,
she gives me her Gmail password

and I scroll through hundreds, find an email
she sent to herself

on the night
on the night
oh my god, on the night of homicide.

He died at 0340.

It is short.
Exacting.
Precise.

He died at 0340.

This is jarring. It could be a nurse's note on a chart. Later—

remember how everything becomes later—I will ask how could you write that and together we will unpack insanity, the slippage, the brief grab back at sanity as she did what she has always done. An obsession for neatness, a compulsion to record events in her journal, document every detail. The carryover to a profession demanding an exact entry for everything whether it be a feeding or a hepatitis shot. *Besides, Mom, crime shows always try to figure out the time of death*; all this crashing against the walls of her cortex as she labors to enter into the record with accuracy. And so on and so forth,

> she entered her son's real name
> (not *He* which I use to protect the innocent).

> My teeth pound. My eyeballs spin.

> How did she find the keyboard in her stupor.
> How could she type.
> How could she.

> "I've always found if I examine something,"
> Joan Didion wrote, "it's less scary."

> I disagree.

MASH-UP

The day after I visit my daughter in prison, I think of what I did
that evening: went to the symphony where the soloist
played a French horn concerto.

> Long ago, my daughter played flute.
> She was in the school band.

On Memorial Day, she marched with the band, playing tunes to

celebrate freedom. I stood on the curb, clapping for those who
went to war for ideals.

On her home front with her son, different battles, paradoxes—*how
can I be so happy when I am so sad*—when her little boy crawls in her lap
to read books, the new neighborhood bereft of neighborliness, how he
shows her each foot in the bathtub, a storm growing with hormonal
shifts and lists, breast is best, she cooks his organic green beans with
compulsion, reads Facebook fictions of motherly perfections, there's no
time to swim with the Wisconsin Athletic Club membership she bought
him, she does not want to be gone from him fifty hours a week—she
wants to be a stay-at-home Mom—how cute he is in the lion costume she
chose for Halloween, she drives into traffic the wrong way and tells no
one, the paranoia of imperfection, at midnight she irons his shirt, did she
get it just right for his holiday photo . . .

   it was a mash-up, a smash-up

   never-good-enough/depressed/wicked anxiety suppressed

         worsened by weaning, hormones gone mad

               friends forfeited, her heart racing to keep up, cook well,
meet demands of a steely boss, give up sleep can't sleep anyway

   while she hurried from and before and around and behind and after

a fiancé fueled by nicotine, sweets, and coffee
      racing past his House of Corrections past
into fulltime work, fulltime school, Saturday overtime
      singing to the boy of his dreams, buying him
a toddler drum set, swishing the sticks with him,
      short-changed on sleep,
the ghost of a ragtag hungry childhood
      coming up the back stairs.
         He's *my* baby, he'd say . . .
         He's *my* baby, she'd say . . .

a refrain I heard fluctuate from cute and playful, to bold and serious.
    I thought it odd, curious—never imagined it was the prologue
for a custody clash, both eager for a child to fulfill them.

    Meanwhile, the fiercest winter since 1936 raged on.

A bad winter for suicides, said the detective, later, flatly,
in the slot of air between us in the squad car when she interviewed me
        after my daughter (high-functioning, the jail psychiatrist would write),
faced a job loss and mounting bills
before she killed once, intent to kill again—herself—after

    her fiancé   ran   out.

His departure, said the expert on filicide,
recreated the horror—the helpless, hopeless, powerless
horror—of her sad-eyed Papa running away
when she was twelve.

                            And before she tried to run away,
                                she wrote a note.

    Mom,

    Thank you for everything you have done for me.
    You have been a wonderful mother and did everything
    in your power. Do not beat yourself up please.

                            Love,
                            Nora

I am powerless.
This love for her impossible,
inexorable.

8 JOB DESCRIPTION

A day after my visit, clouds hang heavy as death
when I swear I hear
that surgeon at Froedtert Hospital tell her,
    I don't rally around my team—my team rallies around me.

He was the boss, dontcha know, didn't everyone know.

And how could she rally   to stay   at work
    until eight pm like he demanded
    when day care closed at six
    when the fiancé attended night school
                and so she couldn't stay, she said
                and so on Friday the 13th, he said
    You're fired as soon as I find a replacement.

        A replacement to stay late, to enter his damn data
        because he refused to learn   electronic charting.

For three months
no replacement could be found, and in the mean meantime
she went to work in one raging snowstorm after another,
going and coming, navigating the locks of her life

in a profession demanding precision, her job description
being written and revised day by day, a new role to pair
a more educated RN (rather than a medical assistant) with a doctor,
a legal requirement for electronic charting.

Anger is stuck in my throat like grimy old pasta stuck to the wall.
And because I'm the Mom and Oma,
    I put on my apron and get out a pot.
    I've always been a great cook.
The pot rages with disorder, ignorance,
        intimate terrorism—look it up—judging tongues,

and empty helping hands, empty
aside from mine.

On the stove, the stew of anger bubbles and boils
    but it is missing a secret ingredient, hers:

I wanted to die
and
I didn't want to leave him behind.

MORNING

Every morning I wake up
with a fresh case of missing

death can do that
set up a turn key

that cannot unlock

while I search for you
eyelids low with longing

if I experience a trauma
over which I have no control

I circle the post
from the past to the present

in the morning
in the evening

you know where you are
and I—I am dreaming

a'ban•don•ment

The day
>after I see her life in prison
>after the last domino fell
>after a life of abandonment
the word abandoned is lost on me.

When a child loses something, she does not forget.
She asks why it is not there, like, for example, her Papa.
She asks why a lot. And how.
For example, how could he do that?

>I too ask why and how and what does abandonment mean?
>Maybe the dictionary will help. It's a start. It says

>(Of a person) having been deserted or cast off.
>Cease to support or look after.
>Give up completely.
>Leave decisively, especially as an act of survival.

An act of survival? Whose, I ask you, Dictionary of Defined Facts
with your detached affect. What's your point of view?
What does it feel like for the one who left? For the one left behind?
Can you define a hard sound beginning behind my daughter's heart
banging every rib
an attack from the inside
when shock took up shop
and never moved out. What was that like?

I wonder what my daughter would say. And so I ask. She writes back.

>*Abandoned is a feeling.*
>*That's what I felt*
>*when I sunk to my knees*
>*when my fiancé walked out*

57

that winter night.
It's a horrible, anxiety-ridden feeling in the pit of my stomach.
Only someone
who has been abandoned numerous times
knows
what this feels like.

"The wound is the place where light enters you," wrote Rumi.
My daughter's light can blind you.
Mine will find you.

LOOK UP

Whether I will it or not, it turns summer
her first in prison
and she calls me to remind me tonight is the full moon

and says, Please Mom, stay up
and look up, see if you see him. She
talks very, very quickly,
others are listening, hesitation in her tone

hurried, how she cannot look up, not after med pass,
not after being locked in to lie in her top bunk.

It is the Harvest Moon except the sky stumbles
in clouds. I stand alone beneath our cathedral ceiling
staring out of massive window panes, so-called picture
windows

watching clouds scud across
as I talk to him, ask him to talk to me.

My view is smeary, though, sketched with haze.
There is no luminosity. Something makes me stand
and wait, how long, I do not know. I would wait

forever for him in dead quiet, lost, transfixed by the
jagged dark, here and there a pockmark of pale light.
I wait some more—what else is there now
but wind and photographic memory.

And then, an opening, a craggy hole where the white wafer
plays hide and seek until lacy clouds light up
and spill the full moon. It bulges

plump cheeks and a melting smile:
my little man-in-the-moon . . . there, here!

I take a photo as proof I am not making
this up.

9 BLUE MILK

When her Papa was on his deathbed

I brought him *The New Yorker*
and opening it, he said
The colors are too vivid now—I can't look.

He narrowed his eyes
his manner restless and fierce. He flipped the pages in the magazine
like years going by, then shut it the way, I imagine,

the prison door shuts
on our daughter on her top bunk
(the penthouse, she calls it)
where she closes her eyes and can't stop
seeing the same scene over and over

> *I just got done screaming*
> *and sobbing*
> *harder than ever.*
> *I miss my baby so much.*

How many times she fed him her thin blue milk, and afterward, carried
him around the house in Good-Night-Moon style, not to say goodnight
but to say hello to his Opa's oils and watercolors, and her
little boy pursed his lips, blinked, took in every brushstroke and contour
like a budding student of line, shape, shadow, and light—
a learner who would be her sunflower for all seasons.

Now, she writes of dour days,
boils on her face, stale air with a taste of asphyxiation,
the photos of him she keeps

> *Sometimes I can't look*
> *That photo of him in the bath: I don't remember taking it*
> *I miss him so much*

How did this happen

her searing story
of believing
in fairytales

now a horror
and
I want you
to remember she wanted
to be more
than this

to be more than the first to feel a miracle
cells multiplying from size of a poppyseed to sesame
then on to a blueberry, grape, lemon and avocado
coming to feed us joy and simplicity

how that little boy tried to remind us

What's important.
What's important.
People, What's Important?

And she, the first there at the end

a screaming hush, shaking, nauseous
the artist's brush muddied
colors bleeding into one another
deprived of desire, desolate as
when she writes from behind a locked door

I thought
I was trying to save him
from a horrible life
I regret it and wish I could go back
I cannot stand how much I miss him.

Bowing my head,
    his larger-than-life love
    fuels me.

It will never die
Infinity redefined

Now and forever
Amen

MAKE GOOD

The day after I visit my daughter in prison

I see her slumped shoulders
and hear her opening salvo
    What are you doing here!?
I lean over the squared-off upholstered block separating us
and burrow into her newly medicated eyes
    To see you   I say
And she says
    You didn't do anything bad, you don't belong here
And I say
    I came to see you

to see   and then to hear
of your treeless Christmas Eve, your attempt to disremember
three years earlier, your lover on his knees, proposing

and she tells me of her current Christmas Day
her sobbing so convulsive
    I almost ended up in obs
obs being the super bright cell for those shrouded in dark

And she feels queasy, stabbed by neck spasms and migraines, recalling

I should have taken a photo or recorded him walking.
I was so out of it, it never occurred to me.
His first steps taken two days before he died, a memory frozen now
as icicles and new snow though snowballs and snow angels
not allowed in the yard, nor stealing

in fact, her schizophrenic cellmate received
a conduct report for sneaking out a donut stick from the cafeteria

Pilfered goods
borrowed dreams

the weight we hand
one another
to ascend above fear
shame
and regret

That's what we are doing
here.
Trying to make good.

EPIGENETICS

In the Netherlands of 1940
running away was not an option
not after Nazis bomb Rotterdam
not after Nazis take away bicycles
not after Nazis leave only bread and water

to feed Elisabeth, belly swollen with her fourth child. She shivers, shakes
while the fetus swims in
faint sounds of blood flushing brand-new ears
the pitch and roll of sleepless nights
a battle through the birth canal

before he—who will become my husband—arrives
    beneath fires across the sky
        crying between bombers
            screaming at shrapnel.

Elisabeth hugs him. She covers his ears.
    But he can still hear his heart.
    It beats like a black bird.
    He thinks it is trapped.
After the war, starving, he is sent to a fattening camp in England.

Paranoia alters his DNA. How could I know he would pass
    twisted strands on to our first-born, a girl.
Fiery despair, always scared. Please Papa, she pleads, stop.
But goose-stepping thoughts keep kicking both their heads.
I dress their wounds.
           Yet there will be no satisfying
           muscle cells, fat cells, blood cells keeping score

he must flee, the Hunger Winter, the runt of the litter.
He becomes fighter, in and out of schools, head pounding
    with migraines, high-strung, healers of no avail.

Then, off to sea at age fifteen, hot-headed and prickly, a Merchant
Marine tramping across the Atlantic to America, arriving in Houston, an
immigrant who
cannot speak the language
    cannot read how to take the next step
        cannot read his own body

                He cannot know what he wants
                until he does what he is doing.

And so, he learns to read the water, he's Dutch in the lap of waves,
storms of deep feeling. He sails Long Island Sound, studies at The Art
Students League, a painter of watercolors with a history of Van Gogh in
his bones.

He leans toward rebel, rogue, and rascal
Awash in danger ... and
   desire
   detachment
   bolting at the sound of thunder and jets.

His view distorted at every turn, tentative, scared to death,
brawling for his very life, panic-stricken by the paranoia
of war—who to trust, why is that person doing that—and I see, too late,
paranoid thinking her marker too, abysmal gloom, gnawing interior
discomfort.

This is the Neuroscience of Epigenetics.

People who live through trauma are changed
in a cellular way. The expression of their DNA, modified,
shows up in subsequent generations, something called
transgenerational trauma, I learn and I observe, dismayed.

   The Nazis did not die.
   Their madness marched on
      genetic memory
      passed along
         like a dropped bomb
     links to violence, my daughter
      born with traumatic residue, a chronic sense of being
unsafe in her body. Many said she was just like her Papa.
     Her hyper vigilance became
a minefield way when her Papa left ... ignited again when the fiancé
left ... and now, hard-wired to panic, feeling unsafe in prison, she writes
       I still don't understand how this place works.

She lives with low expectations, bereft of choice.   She must never run
because, the C.O. tells me, running in prison means
something bad
   is, has,
   or will happen.

She may run in place, however,
on a treadmill   where she can't get very far.

In other words, Mom, I am being institutionalized.

10 SOMEONE ELSE

One of those days after visiting
(does it matter which), it hits me. Kerpow!
I can't keep the lid on anger.

Here I thought it had simmered down,
yet it roils back

much like her anxiety, nightmares, trapped tears
and therapies over the years with her insisting
        Nothing Works.
        It's Not Helping.
        No One Is On My Side.

There are many sides to this story, some diving,
some sliding sideways, each shot full of fear.
Fear inflates anger, remember?

Certainly, I remember. However, I must tell you
when I dumped anger in a pot   and boiled it.
I was not afraid. I was sick. And Tired. And Exhausted.

Still, things never go as planned (don't I know)
and sure enough,
in my disorder and daze, someone else showed up—

someone classy and confident
a magnetic personality ready to go to work.
On me.

Hugging me with quiet assurance, she whispered,
        There is another way to be in the world.

When I asked her name,
        she smiled, Empathy.

TRAVELING THROUGH TIME
AT THE SPEED OF GRIEF

Prison time crawls by. Years. Leftovers of 45 different cellmates—toenail
   fungus, ten black bananas under the bunk, poop on a shared steel toilet,
   socks caked with dirt rolled in a ball and laundered that way, fruit rinds
   withering in heat, the sweaty one who refused showers since she was
   allergic to water—and my daughter cleans up compulsively after them,
   then reads *The Atlantic* and *Smithsonian* and *THE WEEK*, feeding her
   brain. But one article triggers her to remember what she remembered
   when she was booked into the Milwaukee County Jail on suicide watch.

Visions of her village childhood had dawned, events she had long
   forgotten . . . tennis meets, Peppermint Players, eating popcorn with
   her Papa, piano practice . . . memories turbo-charged, one collision
   atop the next too fast to process, all there at the same time.

And then, she remembers what it was she concluded in the jailhouse
   as now she scours her cage, rummaging for a tree-lined life, bicycles,
   swimming at the pool. And in this freefall (how thorns of memory
   poke us as we decay at the end of life), she writes the aftermath of a
   psychotic break:

Vivid, crisp scenes came at me in jail when I realized
what I had done.
My whole life
like a slideshow flashed before my eyes.
This is when I officially died inside.

We call the walking dead, ghosts.

Except when we call them prisoners, those who sweep the floor of
regret
with their hands
      and beg to use the spray bottle with disinfectant to spray away
      shame, a bottle the guards guard like a life depended on it.

ALL ALONG

Pretty soon (or rather, ugly soon), my hands
quiver if I gesture.
A tremor, says
a friend who plods around with me.

She's the first to notice me shake like a drunk
grasping a glass to self-medicate.
I shake when trying to write, text, or type
my twitching a nerve gone nuts.

I worry what it means. Looming disability? Fatal illness?
Trembling, I resolve to find out why.

I try first with finding my feelings—emotional upheavals drop insight,
right?
Well, that doesn't calm my tremor.
Next, I try with intellect—cognition computes insight, right?
Not exactly; it computes a lot of data, overload, overthinking.

Well then, if
neither feelings nor intellect can guide me,
what on earth can?

I wish to find me, the one I used to know.

This requires stillness.
This requires listening.
To myself.

And when I do, I find I have no longer lost me inside myself.
It has been there all along.
It is called
A Body. Mine.

Can I return to living in it
rather than out of it?

69

THE SECRET OF THE THIRD ZONE OF THE SOLAR SYSTEM

"Nothing happens until something moves."
                    -Albert Einstein

Weariness is a malady, heavy and drab. Whether I think
    by feeling or feel by thinking, I am erratic and scattered
        by blasts of advice

from doctors, lawyers, reporters, naysayers,
    jailers and relatives
        knocking me off center.

All this emotion.
        E-motion—it's built into the word.
            Intuitively, I know I gotta move

and keep moving. On the dance floor! I can barely walk
    so how can I tour this dense light
        broken in pieces, wreckage, rubble.

The robust flush I once knew
    with my best dance partner—my second and last
        husband—dimmed the day my daughter

was sentenced and he told me to move. Out.
    And move I do across a smooth maple floor
        crystal chandeliers winking

when you there latch your hip to mine
    and you there slip under my skin like wings
        and you there smile with each footfall.

My shoes are open-toed. I trust your steps, all of them
    from all of you as bones of respect
        beckon my soul.

And it remembers happy. Around the floor it spins
    in a grand embrace of tempo and time,
        alive neither in what happened nor in what's next

but in now, this moment when thighs and fingertips meet
    in the wrap and ringer, rousing a rollout,
        that old razzle-dazzle making heat, madly.

11 BLUEBIRD

My daughter in prison plays the piano.
She plays from memory, eyes closed,
her heart a violin stringing along
as piano notes fall like raindrops
soft while cedar trees and tulips
bend to her allure
there are movements
musical interludes
her long fingers barely touch
one key before alighting on the next
rolling up and down, a lift
at first playful and easy, then loud
in a key of meaning while low sun warms the floor
and lingers like a kiss
a yearning
for something called love.

Enliven it now, that memory, pick up the pace.
    See her at the Young Chang
as I round the corner and pull into the driveway
a twelve-year-old practicing on the upright
so I do not park my heart at empty but at a
home flowing with Sonatina in G Major by Beethoven
a girl making music after her father ran away.

Except. She is only pretending
I will learn, much later, how the blue bench cushion
became a launch pad to an alternative universe
somewhere between fear and possibility as she plucked
at ragged sheet music in grief, threadbare shame,
composed in a little cell with her life
little now, safe and contained and cruel, and family
claiming they can't fix anything, fade into silence.

Musicians say it is the notes not played that make the song.
Meanwhile, my daughter splices quarter-notes with eighths,
off-key, a symphony of stones, a cacophony
as by now I imagine—wouldn't you?—she pounds
each key with fury
a bluebird fighting a crow for the last speck.

ROLLING THOUGHT

The day after I visit
my daughter in prison

I recall how she looked when I saw her
auburn hair curling down her back,
eyes sweetly defined with mascara and shadow,
skin cleared of jailhouse boils, and

    when I told her how startled I was to find
    her brother
    stumbling upon him
        in a dark place—as he put it—a place where thoughts waver
and swirl, looking for a way out. Styron's "storm of murk." Have you
ever found someone in darkness, the dark at the bottom of the ocean where
there is no lucidity, no words. Where my son could not say it but

    We-Are-A-Prison-Family-Now
    over her condition, over the newfangled rules, over the dire distance,
    over recorded phone calls and
    no more texting, family dinners, Snapchat, Facebook

      Enough! Stop! I got it, Mom, she says

opening her pores to agony
her porcelain skin cracking
black stripe of eyeliner running.

My first reaction to her tears was

she did not want to lose him   or
she fretted over him   or
she hoped he would endure the shock of her being sent away.

But instead she whispered
strained and narrow . . . Maybe we could die together.

On my drive home
trucks and cars roared along past
this rolling thought

    Compassion
    means
    something
    else to her

BANANA

I flinch thinking about how she is not allowed to handle money
not even go near the vending machines
in the visiting room so it is up to me to scan
the glass boxes, memorize, and   walk back to her
to ask what she wants—pizza or fries—for
there is no fresh fruit amidst the Cheetos and Skittles

And I remember fruit faraway, of watching her Papa
put a banana peel in the silverware drawer
when I went to be with him in his last Dutch days

at which time he tucked in the peel
with such finesse before taking off all his clothes
then attempted to button an invisible shirt around his swollen
cancerous belly

It was then he turned to me
with a heart-lifting smile and said
    I'd like to do it again
    Only next time
    I'd like to do it better.

In the decade since he died, I ponder 'It'
an elusive pronoun that can function by itself or
partake in discourse: was his 'It' my 'It'? Does it matter as
    past becomes present
    and tomorrow twists memories
    of windsong and longing

    of the whisper paint made
    when it touched his canvas
    and stayed, of
    Beethoven's Triple Concerto
    washing the walls in a Greenwich Village loft
    where I peeled not pages
in a thesaurus but potatoes, where I measured not words but flour,
where I fed not my soul but his as I sprinkled
    powdered sugar on my homemade crepes suzette

Would I do any of it again?
Only if I were crazy

AT THE YMCA

As I'm walking fast
past preschoolers in pink tutus
past Daddys bouncing boys on their knees
past grandmas waiting for class
I keep my head down I want to fight
I'm jealous as I often am
if by accident I spot a mother breastfeeding

75

fixated on her newborn *en face* the nurse
in the birthing center would have noted—the clue
that a miracle of math was born and bonded
super-glued to the mother after the cord cut
because fetal cells will circulate
in her blood for years
I am you and you are me
running in time and the power of touch when serving time
as mothers fathers grandmothers grandfathers
watch kin twinkle off with the YMCA instructor
set foot on the gym floor dance floor pool edge
and I long to sit with them spy be alive
and stop counting on my fingers ankles toes nose
how many gods it will take to guard these little ones
through risk and choice
invisible the promise of chance
neckbones of something called courage

OVERWHELMINGNESS AND WILLINGNESS

It came then to a day of simplicity.
This.

Why you should not talk to me.
Because I cannot listen—nor can I explain things one more time.

Do not fret.

There is much to be done about
sinkholes, volcanic ash, bitterness.

If you do not know what they are
I am sorry for
I cannot stop in this
baffling sniffling slow show,

this mushy in-between
of truth and lies to mention them.

Some things, my very hungry caterpillar,
you must be willing
to unravel

    yourself

until you come
upon
the moment, a metamorphosis

when you realize you can go on, crawling at first,
then lifting your head in pounding waves of humanity,
opening your wings in harsh wind
to achieve lift

see the long view

12 UP OR DOWN

Well, then . . . there comes a time
after I visit
my daughter in prison

when I awaken from dancing
except it is unclear if I am dreaming of dance
or I am the dance, the street light, night tight

It is the same difference I am told the effect
on the brain whether I dance or imagine dancing
Supposedly those who do not or cannot dance
activate pleasure receptors by watching *Dancing with The Stars*

This is hard for me to believe since in every culture
on every continent, people dance—really dance—move it,
shake it, roll it, find the cosmos in their spine and travel it
whether they feel down or up: imagine a
New Orleans cakewalk, an Oneida Pow Wow, Saturday night
polka dances after a day at the plow,
an Irish wake with libation, liquid wrist flicks,
slaves letting loose pelvic rocks and hip clicks
when done with cotton and sugar cane,
country taverns and honky tonks, Ginger Rogers, an ole soft shoe

> And my daughter learns
> how sixty years ago women prisoners
> danced in shirtwaist dresses
> kicking up tie-shoes, leather-soled
> there are photos of such sweet release
> wounds like tattoos rich in art and motion
> the musicality of rhythm and blues, swing.
> Bring it back, I say. I know, I know, no twerking
> no touching of another human allowed
> in today's prison due to PREA
> the Prison Rape Elimination Act

Nonetheless, let everywoman weave her silk, bend her knees freely.
Stop spewing her with hate, disgust of the dark side. She yearns
to rise, shimmy and shine.
She and we are motes of dust in complexity
and contradiction, our beginnings transcend us—why not
too our endings
our toe-tapping to the stars

LAST NIGHT I DANCED THE TANGO

And my partner had air
in his shoes, smooth.

And my waltz partner said
you're a lot of fun to dance with.

And my fox trot partner said
dancing with you is like
driving a sports car.

And all of them held
me in grace
and I was fuel, flame
the energy in my arms
empty with you as I
gathered the music like
a mine-sweeper

      the battle in my heart
      crossing the floor, dodging
      memories of our
      kicks-with-attitude, ronde,
      our seemingly endless
      wrap-turns

before we dipped, tripped

the flint of old hurts flared
    and
when you served
me the papers, your hand touched
mine briefly before

our rollout-to-attack
where we took our positions

and the burn began
    our fiery last Tango close.

HANDS

The day after
I visit my daughter in prison

her downcast face reappears in my brain
like a hologram of the vast visiting room
where I smell burnt air from the microwave
popcorn, pizza, and hot pockets

no sweet smells of peony or rose,
perfumes *verboten*, the Scrabble tiles
between us listless on the board for

    she is staring at her palms
    serious and exasperated
    when she says
    I wish we could hold hands

I open my palms within inches of hers
aware of two correction officers ready to pounce,
to shame affection, prevent a slippage of contraband:

call it a warning
call it a ticket
call it a conduct report
if she touches me
        for there is ceremony here
        rules, a culture of power
        and punishment

She must live inside the razor wire
of fright, yet I must live
in the republic of imagination

And so I wink at her, say
Let's imagine we're holding hands

And we do.
And when we do, I realize I've been holding her, carrying her
   since her Papa disappeared, trying to protect her from further hurt.
And here, I can't protect her anymore much less hug her
though I shall walk next to her,
      our spines bone-deep in back story
      our footfalls merging with the maddening crowd

since "We are all mad here," Lewis Carroll wrote.

LETTERS

The day after I visit my daughter
in prison
      I open my closet and view
      a shelf sagging with the letters

she sends every week
eight to twelve pages
handwritten, printed actually on blue lined paper,
      her brother awestruck by the artistry of her penmanship.

Enclosed, too, are drawings she does six evenings a week
in homage to her little king son
while her cellie begs to see what she's drawing—*I finally yelled at her!*

I imagine my daughter
sitting on her top bunk
crunched forward like at Girl Scout camp
braiding together the day
of
bad food, mean counselors, cagey campers
If you don't come and get me, I am going to die here.

And now, in a letter from prison
her sealed subconscious leaks on to the page
When Papa left, I stopped talking.

Years ago, a therapist told me
she was fine, expressed no concern.

Finally, I know: she could not.

It took twenty-seven years
for a fatherless girl forever
drawn to the desperate and the extreme
to excavate truth
hand-print it in a letter home

My
sadness
was
cemented
in
me
at that time

TIME

The day after I visit
my daughter in prison

I realize it is not the day after.

It is the day before
and four days after.

It is the middle of the night
and it is twilight.

Each is the same now—each
wishing, wanting,
wondering

how she keeps her dignity during the strip search after I leave
the guard on guard,
my daughter on guard, stress chemicals spit the shadows, her cheeks
bend over and cough
cry of my lungs
bony my knees

what drawings will you create this week, what vibrating lines of
color in Zentangles and curlicues, the unraveling of a Gordian knot,
Escher-like clues to healing, Mandalas drawn by the light of your son,
my grandson who so loved the world that he agreed to come

and when did your cellmate stop passing wicked gas, stop
eating all her canteen, stop throwing up, stop flushing the toilet, stop
claiming there was only carbon dioxide in the cell and you were both
going to die

and when did you say
to the next cellmate and the next, please, please,

bloody-well please turn out
the overhead light and

Let Mommy Sleep

PART TWO | MERCY

THE YELLOW TOOTHBRUSH

PART THREE | MOTION

THE YELLOW TOOTHBRUSH

13 WHAT TO DO ABOUT STUFF AND WHEN

The day after I visit my daughter in prison
the air is smudged, bulging with murk and mist

There are many murky days now,
going through photos and cards
misremembering things, her brother and I,

Look at that bracelet, we
guess that was when
or maybe not, gosh, it must have been
another when, you know, when
she did this and I did what
no, you did that and I said
ohmygod, look at that

     And. We. Did.

asking one another
what to do about the easel, sofa, Apple Mac,
HD-TV she just paid off, organic sugar,
queen bed, dressers,
Crate & Barrel tables,
Andrew Weill's holistic and integrative healing hand lotion,
     and that engagement ring, and oh oh,
      what about the organic baby shampoo

would you use
     Seventh Generation Household Cleaner
I'll take the balsamic, you take the organic parsley and cinnamon

As for the leather coat and
White House/Black Market
pants, blouses, and dresses
a consignment shopper will treasure them
     they won't fit me

All the material materials
that once shaped a life

And my son says
 We Are Still In Life
He's always full of elliptical aphorisms,
 the picker-upper, the peacemaker

At least we can keep her jade plant alive and

store stacks of books
with her Book Woman bookplates noting
 This Belongs To _____ (my daughter)

And they still do.

As for the baby shampoo, it isn't
 just for babies, not now, not anymore.

VENERABLE

Dear my Grandson,

 Come and let's rerun a wedding reception playing in four-part harmony, you in bowtie and vest and me in summery skirt, a billowy blouse as we dance, my arms around you like sleeves when we fox trot into an evening endless, tapping and whirling, twirling through generations to come, through long run-on sentences because we never think it will end, how could it, it is only beginning, it is only Rumi believing God likes us when we sing but loves us when we dance and I believe you—my joy, my boy—will dance all night, will see more at the reception than I, will gaze on one florid face after another, every flower, each piece of cake and glittery glass, goofy DJ,

and you can't yet talk but you take in—through every clap and kiss,
every whiff of perfume, so please tell me: what is it you love and will
keep on loving, what is it.

Your Oma,
Kathryn

THE RESHAPING OF CONSCIOUSNESS

The days when I visit my prisoner daughter
I learn the colors: olive for officers and sergeants
white for lieutenants and captains

military-style shirts embroidered with
Wisconsin Department of Corrections.
Excuse me, but no one can correct

how a neighbor said she looked very calm
(pale, listless, two nights without sleep)
handcuffed, shuffling to the squad car

armed guards then stationed at her E.R. bed
to keep her from wanting to die while detectives
combed her house after she signed a search warrant

the officer's pen could be a ribbon for all she knew
suicide notes found neatly arranged on the landing,
passwords, file folders for home, car, health,

student loan, immunizations, coupons,
two diaries/one for baby/one for fiancée:
every fact way laid, to be backtracked

after she's caged and off to the cop shop at two am
waiving her Miranda rights before talking
and talking and talking, the dam of an introvert burst

I was desperate that's why I was with him
the dehumanization in place, slow spin
moves and crossovers reshaping consciousness

14 MEDITATION ON A WALL

Not sure how you get through every day.

This comment or a thousand variations
thrown at me so many times
I lose count

but I can count 200 calls fired at me
from jail, crying Help! Help! Help! That means
Get. Me. Out. Of. Here.

The way to do that is post bail. Wisconsin is a cash-bail state:
a defendant must pay the full amount in order to await trial
outside of jail. Bail, from Latin *bajulare*, to bear a burden,
a burden that becomes mine alone, a stress test for family
ethics, distributive justice, the allocation of resources. I
beseech $100,000 from sympathizers (put your money
where your tongue is) though I learn later—why is it I must
learn, later, always later—that people donate based
on either outcome or passion.

And so, outcome and passion enter the ring. I jab, step-
outside, fake the step-out, duck to the counter, skip to the right
instead of the left. Every move I try, intent to get her out and find
where she can live with psychiatric care while court jesters tack on
one status hearing after another, crawl toward trial, cannot hear *help-
help-help*, surely must know that every wall has two sides and two
stories, fear on one side and understanding on the other.

And I cannot bust down the wall.
I feel like I've sustained verbal whiplashes,
each cry from her a paper cut
thin sharp serious
my legs bleed in spasms
the vice-grip on me unrelenting, wild as a charley horse

broken through the barn door
blood red drips, scratching, gnawing

And you too will ask, how do you get through the day
I know you will . . . and thus, let me tell you how to get
through a day, dusk, midnight, creeping dawn.

Glue your shoes to the floor and walk
out of yourself.

MATHEMATICAL FACT

John Farrow
(Mia Farrow's father)
was born February 10, 1904.

Shortly thereafter,
his mother
(Mia Farrow's grandmother)
was institutionalized
for what was
then called
Lactation Psychosis.

She died in the institution.

Do the math.
One hundred and ten years
of mothers
crying.
For help.

DIZZY

The day after
      I visit my daughter
            in prison
                  I feel dizzy.

And there is no one to catch me.
I should move, I think,
find a place with catchers.

So I move
into the back brain.
It is a place with tunnels and gears,
a strong rope, and an interesting
device with a bubble
      in the middle like a level.

My back brain, responsible for
      balance
      and
      coordination,
levels with me.

It does not
care
to know
why
I moved.

Why has nothing to do with balance.

How, does.

15 TELLING THE TRUTH

The hardest part of telling the truth
is telling the truth.

In all truth, there are those who stopped loving her.
They didn't tell me.
I saw it in their faces.
A way to cope. Shun. Dodge.

The hardest part of telling
the truth is telling the truth.

In all truth, I too wished to run
away. It seemed a matter of self-preservation.
You can choose to be happy, I was told.
Move on, was a phrase thrown at me many times.
Besides, people fall out of love every day.
It's the Humpty Dumpty of the human condition.

I wanted to fall so far I would think I dreamt it all,
fall so far that all the king's horses and all
the king's men couldn't put me back together again.

And then, my daughter learns that most prisoners
are forgotten five years in. Forgotten? Is that a way of falling?

Can one ever forget falling in love?
Can one fall and be caught, only to fall again?
What breaks when you fall? What breaks the fall?

Falling in love with a child is unlike any other fall.
It starts at the moment of miracle and slips and slides
faster when the child appears, cheesy and
red-faced, bawling to beat the band.
It circles preschool high school and university, takes on annoyance

when the testing comes and can either deepen or dry out
from disappointment.

The hardest part of telling the truth is telling the truth.

And so, the farther I fell, love's trickery fell with me.
And as I was about to move on, loving her less, I realized I loved her more.

Sometimes things are unbearable and yet they have to be born.

MADISON

The day after I visit my daughter in prison

I walk the streets of Madison, the University,
Henry Street leading me past the popular
Tau Kappa Epsilon house,
international party time with
people on porches, the Plaza Tavern
and next door to that, a sudden sign:

WI State Public Defender Office

I walk faster, past it, past all that.

Earth-tone leaves from last night's
stormy trees
stick to the sidewalk, the wind a soft hum
the sound of angel wings
teasing each leaf to take off.

Lift, waft, turn, blow.
One leaf at a time lets go.

I am so in love with life
I must be mad.

97

CHRISTMAS

The day after I visit my
daughter in prison
I stare at the Christmas
card she sent.

It is mid-January, raining,
earth mother without her coat of snow.

Snow. The pure white stuff.
So simple and vital.
A primal rebirth
        how to begin again
        start over.

        Her holiday card
rests on my desk, her hands
fashioned it by gluing together
red and green construction
paper, grade-school grade, and
then crimping it in half
so the outside is green, the inside redder
than the lining of an artery.

The creek outside my window swells, furious,
a rage of rain.

        Inside the card, my daughter wrote
with a green marker,
all caps in her artistic bubble printing

MOM, THANK YOU FOR STILL LOVING ME.

Sleet beats the window. Rain bangs for kindness.
This homesick winter yearns for cozy cold snow.

Love is a curse, this I know.
Mother love is a crazy blessing, this I thank.

THE TRAIN

Not the next day
nor the next night
but every night
a train trundles past

near midnight
        its whistle winding
            through the lowland

past darkened windows
of homes where someone is leaving
someone else arriving
        in the loopy black
            clatter of commotion

the tracks safely laid for travelers to travel
arrive where they can
lie down next to
or away from want

        and awaken refreshed
        on the other side of

comprehension
where they hear the echoing
of an all-knowing crone, a very grand mother,
her belly unbuttoning
age-old advice

her refrain resounding

Forgiveness dawns in the night

one dimension slides into another
trilling high above a hard sky
recognizing the past could not have been
any different

It is inexplicable, invisible,
how we love. And when.

16 DINNER PARTY

Setting the table
I count the number expected
thanks to social graces

of those who responded, who will come for

sweet potato lentil soup
arugula salad with grapefruit and pistachios
beef brisket and spaetzle dumplings
drunken peaches and cream

And I hum as I smooth the tablecloth,
arrange the centerpiece and candlesticks
polish the silver before placing

knife, spoon, soup spoon
to the right of each Delft Blue plate
dinner fork and salad fork to the left

dessert spoon posed horizontally
above, a crowning touch,
the taste of final sweet gazing at

salt and pepper shakers in Waterford crystal
water glasses winking at wine goblets
the scent of baby roses, low, for conversation

when suddenly, the tune in my head changes
and I make room for one more setting
of plate, knife, forks, and spoons

fold another napkin into a shape wistful as a kite
and then, about to set a dessert spoon for that final touch,
I hesitate and return the spoon to its place

in the drawer where it will nest between delight
and despair because her face
is the only dessert my dinner party needs

GRACE

The day after I visit my daughter in prison

I can see her brows in jagged fury
arms crossed, crimson neck flushed in fear.
Nothing I can do about any of it.

It is Friday, time to put on my red lace dress
and black leggings,
drive to the dance hall

where I keep changing partners:
a shy newcomer, one seasoned,

a man from Calgary who could waltz
waltz me across the continent

a rumba hold ignites an erotic high
and a fall-away twinkle in Fox Trot
O! Oh! What can I say when

a fire in my belly burns
and I gyrate, loop-and-split,

flick, kick, twist, and trap
make a pretzel or
rubber band move
power up muscle memory
ions and proteins
to make
a sugar push, the sweetest mood.

Music has phrases.
Courts have sentences.
A sentence to me is
      subject
      verb
      direct object
with punctuation at the end.

Woman. Sentenced. First-degree reckless.
Twenty-five years. No early release due to truth-in-sentencing.
An exclamation gavel or two from a judge
in the dark about perinatal mood disorder—he called it Evil—   his time
finite like all of us.

And I shall dance in his court
not as jester or bayonet

        but as hour hand, time ticking

              the sound of a first
                heartbeat
                 faint
              as the last

Tragedy plus time equals comedy
my comedienne friend says

at one time my daughter's laugh
rolled from her toes, her wit sharp and quick,
she had more than one funny bone when she laughed
uproarious, hilarious how the phrase

'time immemorial' means so long ago that
      people have no knowledge or memory of it
while depression takes its own time

how can I not bandage her wound with mine?

tell her it's going to be all right when it won't
        not now
not in this life cocked and loaded with
        panic
        terror and transgression
        cruelty and lies
all of which I don't know
what to do about, except

ache, transform, make art, trace
every beat of infinite heat
into a happy-sad-mad-glad dance

dance for her
dance for everyone hurt, betrayed, or lost.

Dance like a dervish
whirl in form, howl in beauty,
hum an old song unheard of.

LIMELIGHT

Movement is mystic
a gift

And so, accepting the gift
I step into the limelight
        fervent to find
        the time of my body
        the line of my soul

I move in octaves and intervals
possibilities for small
but intense points of
intimacy

until the music stops
until

I stumble
and fall

black and blue
yellow and red
white, pale

in pieces

yet I hear
one more note
one more measure

calling me to be
more than hostage
to the madness

and so I dance
and need to dance
rapturous and ready
to see her face
freed

. . . a body to carry me into this world,
through the birth-cries and the love-cries, too

-Kim Addonizio
"What Do Women Want?"

All things come to an end.
No, they go on forever.
-Ruth Stone

ACKNOWLEDGEMENTS

I would like to thank patience, a virtue to evade me as I sought courage to speak truth and then a publisher with verve to publish it. Now that you are here, dear reader, you know patience came through—as did Two Shrews, including acquiring editor Jordan Leon.

I am grateful, too, for family and friends who accompanied me. First and foremost, my daughter Nora Zylstra whose dream unraveled, my son Owen Zylstra whose vein of compassion ran deep, my brother Jon Freis who stood like a sentinel at my side as I fielded phone calls, my sister Mary Ann Schnur who knew what to say and when, my sister Lisa Vanden Avond whose tears bathed the wounds of the soul and my nephew Joe Vanden Avond for his exemplary empathy.

Heartfelt thanks to Bob and Holly Johnson for circling me with age-old wisdom and grace. Thank you, Dianne Parisi for showing up at my door with a red Talbots blazer, wrapping me with care every time I wore it. To Ellen O'Brien and Dixie Zittlow, illumination from mothers with intense loss. And to forever friends, Mike and Maxine Olson, who steadied me with their calm demeanor.

Deepest gratitude to Valerie Krejcie for unwavering attention and for taking me away on the California Zephyr when I needed perspective, distance. Special praise to the late Cheryl Bornemann, best cousin and librarian extraordinaire. High regard for women warriors like Ann Allen, erudite stagehand in the theater of the mind, Joyce Atkins decoding family history, and Sharon Reilly opening her mouth like a bird to heal me. Sandie Honl checked on me like a steady pulse. Carol Fitzmaurice extended her R.N. lifeline. I would not have made it without David McCreanor, too, his earthy guidance, nor without Craig Blumer, an angel who waltzed me through a maze. Unique gratitudes to Karl Elder, a shining captain in the storm and to Tara Pohlkotte, who brought me to Storycatchers stage, to Janene Israel for researching grandmothers like me, and to Katayune Kaeni for my appearance on *Mom & Mind*. And of course, indebtedness to writers who listened, including Sarah Sadie, my first reader and then Kathryn Walczyk, Jean Biegun, Sylvia Cavanaugh, Georgia Ressmeyer, Dawn Hogue, Blair Deets, Lisa Vihos, plus the splendid Kim Klein and Amy Mazzarillo. Countless others encircled me with kindness. Because of so many, I am still here, dreaming.

•

Gratefully acknowledged are the editors and curators of the following where forms of these vignettes first appeared:

CALYX: A Journal of Art and Literature by Women: "Bed," "Cloudy," "Her Yesterday Face"

Intersections: Art and Poetry: "Morning"

New Millennium Writings: "Banana"

Rosebud: "The Institute"

Storycatchers: "I Am Going to Lose My Mind"

The Mill Prize: "With Other Mothers"

Studio One: "Underwater"

The Baltimore Review: "Sunrise in May"

vividly, the beauty of consciousness: "Overwhelmingness and Willingness"

Wisconsin People & Ideas: "Bluebird"

CALL TO ACTION

In March of 2014 Nora Zylstra, a new mother silently suffering from anxiety, severe depression, OCD, and paranoid thinking took the life of her son. Immediately after, she tried to commit suicide, but did not succeed.

If she had done this in Illinois or Massachusetts, or more than two dozen countries, including Canada, Nora would have gone to a mental health facility. Instead, it happened in Wisconsin and she was sentenced to prison for twenty-five years.

One in five pregnant or postpartum women experience depression, anxiety, or scary thoughts, according to the American College of Obstetricians and Gynecologists (ACOG). In low socioeconomic communities, the numbers rise to one in four. For most, the disorder recedes. For the undiagnosed/untreated, it can worsen—for up to two years after giving birth. Only 19% of those who need help seek help due to stigma or racial or ethnic disparities in the use of mental health services.

When Nora became lucid enough to realize what she'd done, she was devastated. She is still devastated, but with time, medication, therapy, and a mother who did not give up on her, she is finding her way back.

Like many mothers in the United States, Nora deserved better. Mothers with postpartum disorders deserve mental healthcare before they arrive at a crisis point, not punishment. They deserve compassion, mercy, and a place to go to heal and find peace, where their families can visit freely to support them. It is a clear miscarriage of the concept of justice that where an event takes place has so much to do with the outcome of the case and the future of the person involved.

If you would like to sign a petition to state legislators who have power to change laws for women suffering from perinatal or postpartum mood and anxiety disorders (PMAD), please join us at change.org/yellowtoothbrush.

•

Postpartum Support International helps pregnant women and new mothers in crisis and lobbies to increase funding for treatment and prevention of perinatal mood disorders. Find out more about their work at postpartum.net.

If you or someone you know needs help, call their helpline at 1-800-944-4773.

ABOUT THE AUTHOR

Kathryn Gahl began writing as a farm girl and kept writing through dual degrees in English and nursing, a career as nurse manger, and mothering a daughter and son, alone. Her fiction, nonfiction and poetry, deeply rooted in everyday life, combine human pathos with quick wit and deeply felt truths.

Her works—appearing in over fifty journals, three anthologies, and six ekphrastic art shows—have won numerous awards, including The Hal Prize for Fiction and Poetry and the Lorine Niedecker Poetry Award. A Pushcart nominee, she received an Outstanding Achievement Award from the Wisconsin Library Association for *The Velocity of Love* (Water's Edge Press, 2020). Cornerstone Press selected *Messengers of the Gods: New & Selected Poems* for its Portage Poetry Series (2022).

An avid ballroom dancer, she believes in the power of dark chocolate, deep sleep, and red lipstick.

ALSO BY KATHRYN GAHL

Life Drawing Class
The Velocity of Love
Messengers of the Gods: New and Selected Poems
Hard Life, Hard Love

ABOUT TWO SHREWS PRESS

Two Shrews is an independent and very selective press inspired by women and girls who, every day, listen to each other and, implicitly or explicitly, talk back to the patriarchy. Two Shrews exists to help them be heard. Based in Green Bay, Wisconsin and New York City, and co-founded by two best friends, our books proudly foster conversation between coastal and middle America.